THE NIGHT BEFORE CHRISTMAS

and Nine Best-Loved Carols

Library of Congress Cataloging-in-Publication Data

Moore, Clement Clarke, 1779-1863.
    The night before Christmas / by Clement C. Moore; illustrated by
Elizabeth Miles.
       p.   cm.
      Summary: A well-known poem about an important Christmas visitor.
    ISBN 0-8167-1209-3 (lib. bdg.)   ISBN 0-8167-1210-7 (pbk.)
    1. Santa Claus—Juvenile poetry. 2. Christmas—Juvenile poetry.
3. Children's poetry, American. [1. Santa Claus—Poetry.
2. Christmas—Poetry. 3. American poetry. 4. Narrative poetry.]
I. Miles, Elizabeth J., ill. II. Title.
PS2429.M5N5 1988
811'.2—dc19   87-15343
                                   CIP

THE NIGHT BEFORE CHRISTMAS

CLEMENT C. MOORE

Illustrated by
Elizabeth Miles

and Nine Best-Loved Carols

Troll Associates

Twas the night before Christmas,
when all through the house,
Not a creature was stirring,
not even a mouse.

The stockings were hung
by the chimney with care,
In hopes that St. Nicholas
soon would be there.
The children were nestled
all snug in their beds,
While visions of sugarplums
danced in their heads;

And Mama in her kerchief,
and I in my cap,
Had just settled our brains
for a long winter's nap,

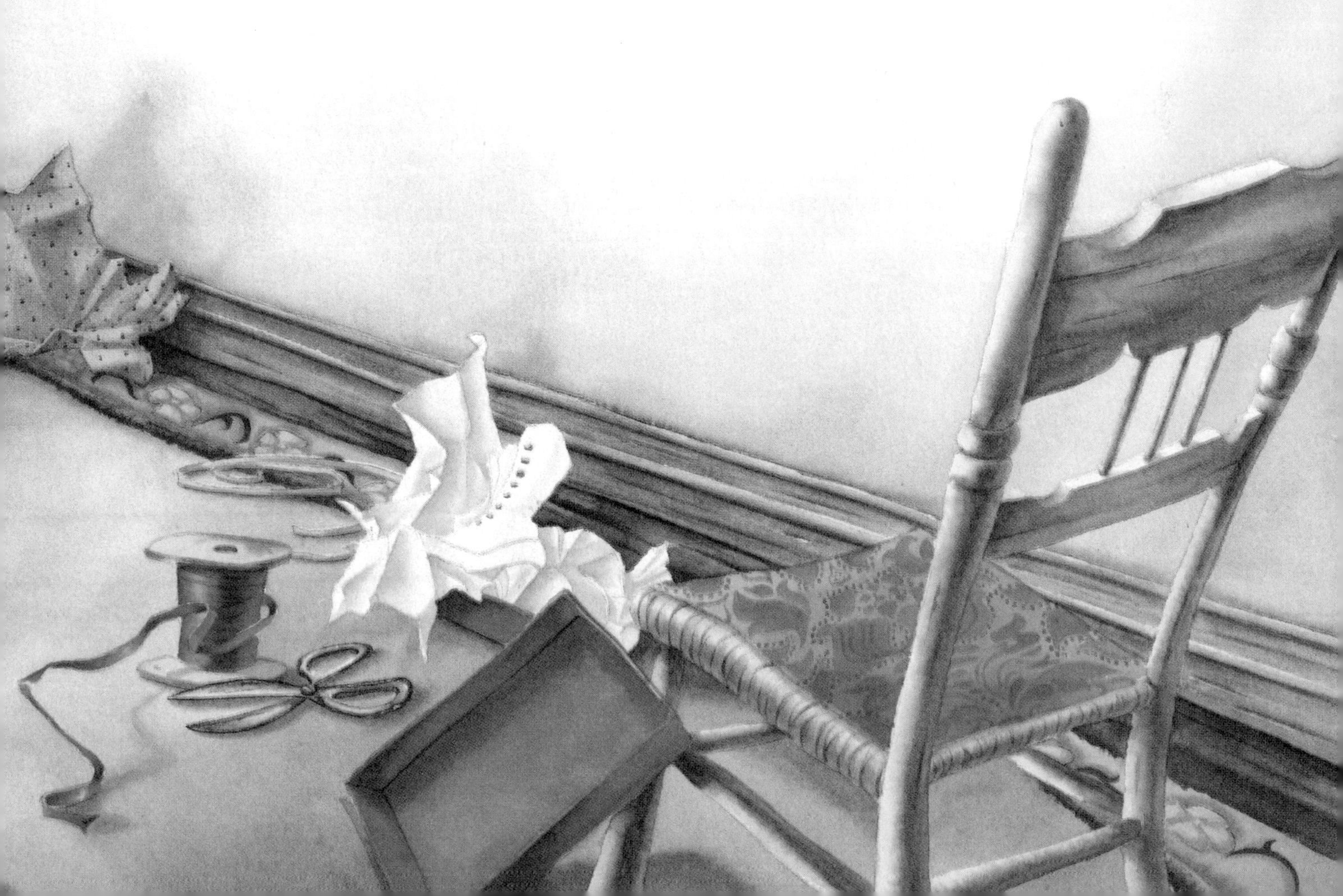

When out on the lawn
there arose such a clatter,
I sprang from my bed
to see what was the matter.

Away to the window
I flew like a flash,
Tore open the shutters
and threw up the sash.

The moon on the breast
of the new-fallen snow
Gave a luster of midday
to objects below;

When what to my wondering eyes
should appear
But a miniature sleigh
and eight tiny reindeer,

With a little old driver,
so lively and quick,
I knew in a moment
it must be St. Nick!

More rapid than eagles
his coursers they came,
And he whistled and shouted
and called them by name:
"Now, Dasher! now, Dancer!
now, Prancer and Vixen!
On, Comet! on, Cupid!
on, Donder and Blitzen!

To the top of the porch!
to the top of the wall!
Now dash away! dash away!
dash away, all!"

As dry leaves that before
the wild hurricane fly,
When they meet with an obstacle,
mount to the sky,
So up to the housetop
the coursers they flew,
With a sleigh full of toys—
and St. Nicholas too.

And then, in a twinkling,
I heard on the roof
The prancing and pawing
of each little hoof.

As I drew in my head
and was turning around,
Down the chimney St. Nicholas
came with a bound.

He was dressed all in fur,
from his head to his foot,
And his clothes were all tarnished
with ashes and soot;

A bundle of toys
he had flung on his back,
And he looked like a peddler
just opening his pack.
His eyes, how they twinkled!
his dimples, how merry!
His cheeks were like roses,
his nose like a cherry!
His droll little mouth
was drawn up like a bow,
And the beard on his chin
was as white as the snow.

The stump of a pipe
he held tight in his teeth,
And the smoke, it encircled
his head like a wreath.
He had a broad face
and a little round belly
That shook, when he laughed,
like a bowl full of jelly.

He was chubby and plump,
a right jolly old elf,
And I laughed when I saw him,
in spite of myself.
A wink of his eye
and a twist of his head
Soon gave me to know
I had nothing to dread.

He spoke not a word,
but went straight to his work,
And filled all the stockings,
then turned with a jerk,
And laying a finger
aside of his nose,
And giving a nod,
up the chimney he rose.

He sprang to his sleigh,
to his team gave a whistle,
And away they all flew
like the down of a thistle.
But I heard him exclaim,
ere he drove out of sight,
"Happy Christmas to all,
and to all a good night!"

Jingle Bells

The First Noël

Moderato

Traditional

2. They looked up and saw a star
   Shining in the East beyond them far,
   And to the earth it gave great light,
   And so continued both day and night.
   (REFRAIN)

3. And by the light of that same star,
   Three wise men came from country far,
   To seek for a king was their intent,
   And to follow the star wherever it went.
   (REFRAIN)

4. This star drew nigh to the northwest,
   O'er Bethlehem it took its rest,
   And there it did both stop and stay
   Right over the place where Jesus lay.
   (REFRAIN)

Silent Night

Franz Grüber / Joseph Mohr

2. Silent night, Holy night,
   Shepherds quake at the sight.
   Glories stream from heaven afar,
   Heav'nly hosts sing "Alleluia."
   Christ, the Savior, is born,
   Christ, the Savior, is born.

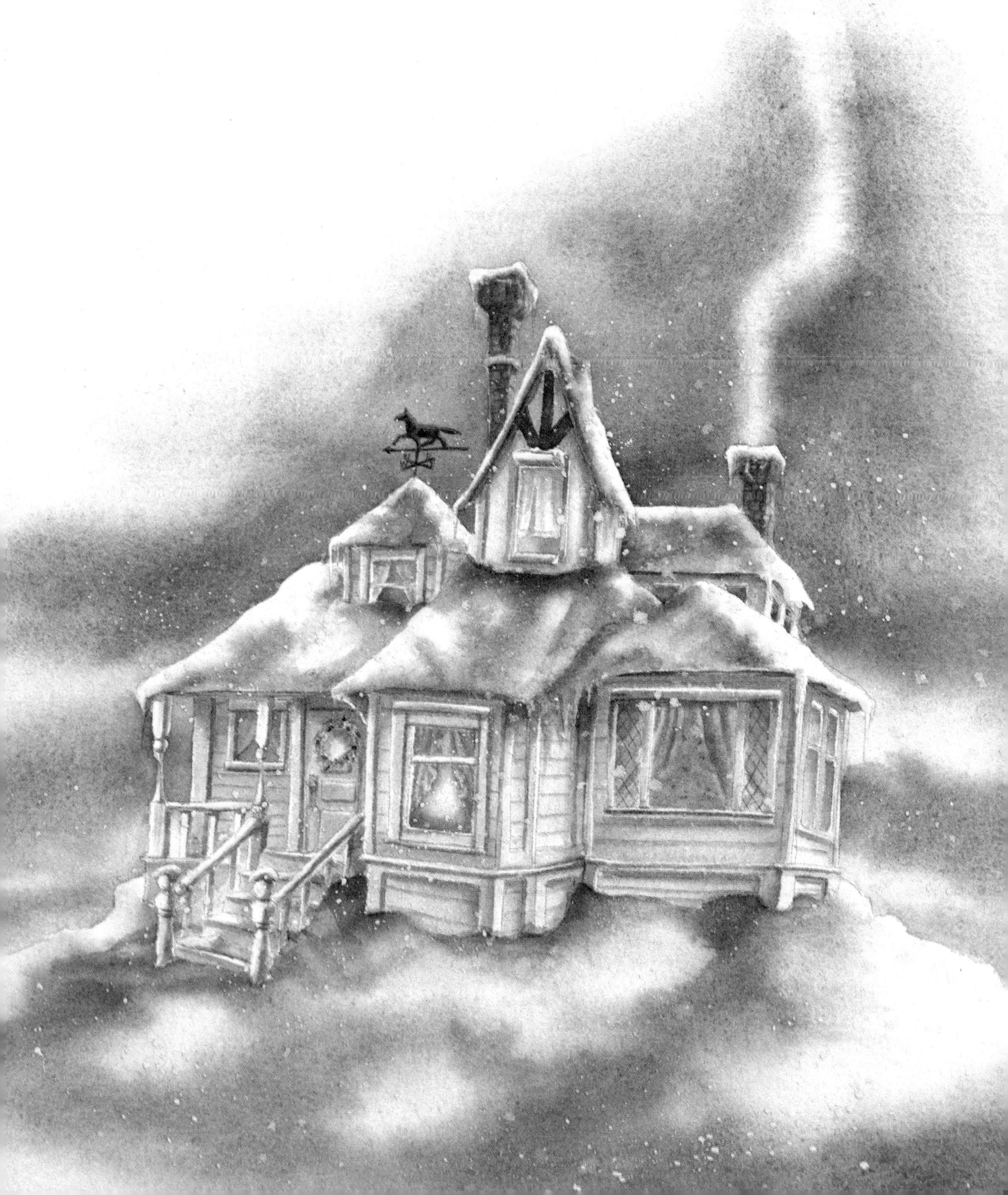

Deck the Halls

Traditional

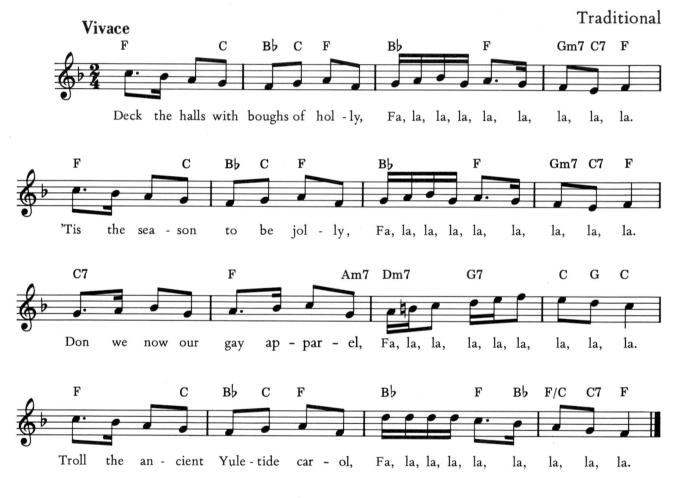

Vivace

Deck the halls with boughs of hol-ly, Fa, la, la, la, la, la, la, la, la.

'Tis the sea-son to be jol-ly, Fa, la, la, la, la, la, la, la, la.

Don we now our gay ap-par-el, Fa, la, la, la, la, la, la, la, la.

Troll the an-cient Yule-tide car-ol, Fa, la, la, la, la, la, la, la, la.

2. See the blazing Yule before us,
   Fa, la, la, la, la, la, la, la, la.
   Strike the harp and join the chorus,
   Fa, la, la, la, la, la, la, la, la.
   Follow me in merry measure,
   Fa, la, la, la, la, la, la, la, la,
   While I tell of Yuletide treasure,
   Fa, la, la, la, la, la, la, la, la.

3. Fast away the old year passes,
   Fa, la, la, la, la, la, la, la, la.
   Hail the new, ye lads and lasses,
   Fa, la, la, la, la, la, la, la, la.
   Sing we joyous all together,
   Fa, la, la, la, la, la, la, la, la.
   Heedless of the wind and weather,
   Fa, la, la, la, la, la, la, la, la.

O Christmas Tree

Traditional

O Christ-mas Tree, O Christ-mas Tree, Thy leaves are so un - chang -ing. O

Christ-mas Tree, O Christ - mas Tree, Thy leaves are so un - chang -ing. Not

on - ly green when sum-mer's here, But al - so when 'tis cold and drear. O

Christ-mas Tree, O Christ - mas Tree, Thy leaves are so un - chang -ing.

2. O Christmas Tree, O Christmas Tree,
Much pleasure cans't thou give me.
O Christmas Tree, O Christmas Tree,
Much pleasure cans't thou give me.
How often has the Christmas Tree
Afforded me the greatest glee.
O Christmas Tree, O Christmas Tree,
Much pleasure cans't thou give me.

3. O Christmas Tree, O Christmas Tree,
Thy candles shine so brightly.
O Christmas Tree, O Christmas Tree,
Thy candles shine so brightly.
From base to summit, gay and bright,
There's only splendor for the sight.
O Christmas Tree, O Christmas Tree,
Thy candles shine so brightly.

4. O Christmas Tree, O Christmas Tree,
    How richly God has decked thee.
    O Christmas Tree, O Christmas Tree,
    How richly God has decked thee.
    Thou bidst us true and faithful be,
    And trust in God unchangingly.
    O Christmas Tree, O Christmas Tree,
    How richly God has decked thee.

Joy to the World

Maestoso

Lowell Mason/Isaac Watts

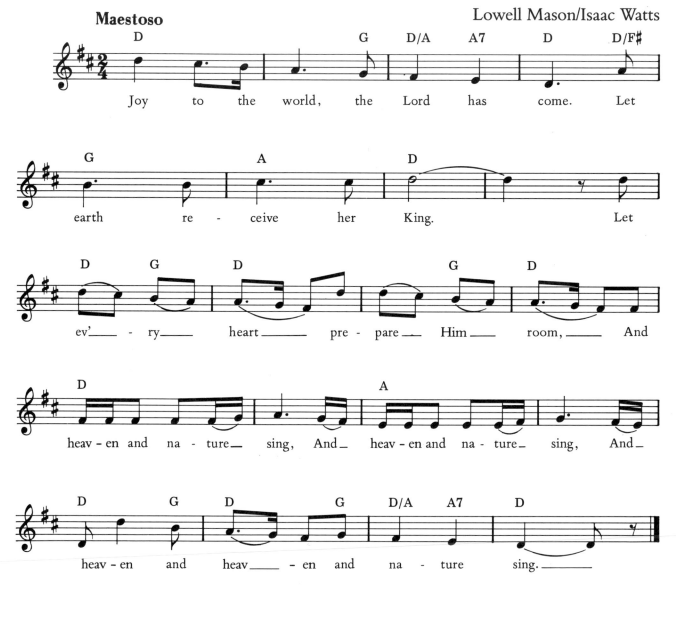

Joy to the world, the Lord has come. Let earth re - ceive her King. Let ev' - ry heart prepare Him room, And heav - en and na - ture sing, And heav - en and na - ture sing, And heav - en and heav - en and na - ture sing.

Hark! The Herald Angels Sing

Allegro

Felix Mendelssohn/Charles Wesley

Hark! The her - ald an - gels sing,— "Glo - ry to the new - born King!

Peace on earth and mer - cy mild,— God and sin - ners re - con - ciled."

Joy - ful all ye na - tions rise,— Join the tri - umph of the skies;—

With an - gel - lic host pro - claim, "Christ is— born in Beth - le - hem."

Hark! The her - ald an - gels sing, "Glo - ry— to the new - born King!"

O Come, All Ye Faithful

Traditional

We Wish You a Merry Christmas

Traditional

Allegro

G   C   A7   D7

We wish you a mer-ry Christ-mas, We wish you a mer-ry Christ-mas, We

B7   Em   G   Am7   D7   G

wish you a mer-ry Christ-mas and a hap-py new year. Good

G   Bm   Em   A7   D7

tid-ings to you wher-ev-er you are; Good

G   Bm   Em7   Am   D7   G

tid-ings for Christ-mas and a hap-py new year. We

G   C   A7   D7

wish you a mer-ry Christ-mas, We wish you a mer-ry Christ-mas, We

B7   Em   G   Am7   D7   G

wish you a mer-ry Christ-mas and a hap-py new year.